SIERRA PERIJÁ AND ORINOCO

Stephen Platt

www.leveretpublishing.com

Sierra Perijá and Orinoco
First published - September 2025
Published by Leveret Publishing
56 Covent Garden, Cambridge, CB1 2HR, UK

Yukpa earrings – chrysanthemum pattern

ISBN 978-1-912460-16-8

SIERRA PERIJÁ 1973

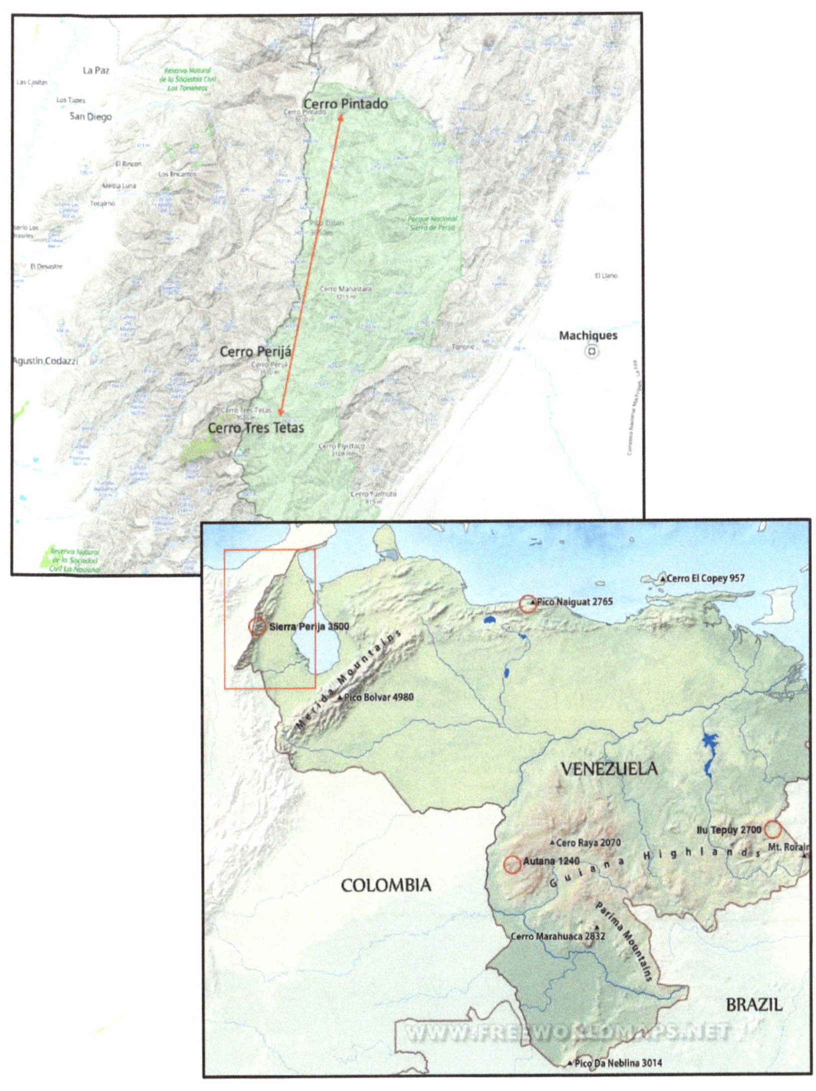

Sierra Perijá

In 1972, I went on an expedition to mark the border along the Sierra de Perijá between Venezuela and Colombia for the Venezuelan Comisión de Fronteras with Daniel Genoud and four Makiritare Indians from the Upper Orinoco.

The Serranía del Perijá is the western spur of the Andes running north–south along the Zulia–Cesar/Norte de Santander frontier. It stretches for 300 kilometres, ending in the Guajira Peninsula and the Gulf of Venezuela. The border was, for various reasons, sensitive. The exact line of the frontier was uncertain, and the mountains were a hot spot in the Colombian conflict and used as a refuge by guerrillas of FARC and ELN. The highest point is Cerro de Las Tetas at 3,630 metres, followed by Cerro Pintado at 3,610 m, Cerro Peijá 3510 m, and Cerro Irapa 2430 m.

It is a complex ecological, cultural, and strategic zone. The mountains are home to Indigenous communities (Yukpa, Barí, and others) whose territories straddle the international border, and the area holds valuable

Sierra Perijá and part of the ridge we traversed

resources, including water, fertile valleys, and coal deposits. The area is home to various large mammals, including the spectacled bear, one of which we saw and the Makiritare tried to shoot, and capuchin and howler monkeys. There are also various endangered bird species, including macaws and hummingbirds.

Spectacled bear Segundo tried to shoot

Plant communities include moist forest with dry forest in drier pockets at lower elevations, montane forest at middle elevations, and subalpine forest at upper elevations, with areas of high, flat plains, páramo (alpine shrubland), and snow-covered peaks at high elevations. It was this paramo landscape of heather-like bushes and coarse grasses that we traversed on our expedition.

Paramo vegetation typical of the ridge we followed

The forests are high in biodiversity with many native species, including endemic and limited-range species. Endemic birds include the Perijá metaltail (Metallura iracunda) and the Perijá brushfinch (Arremon perijanus). Although much of the area is a national park, fires are a significant threat, and there is severe deforestation.

The range is 58% in Venezuela and 42% in Colombia. Venezuela has set aside a substantial part of the central part of the range as a national park (Sierra de Perijá National Park), and Colombia has a smaller one. This area is traditionally the home of the Bari Indians, who were called Motilones or warlike people. In Venezuela, there are Amerindian reservations for the Yukpa and Barí people. The climate is tropical, with humid forests at lower altitudes, favouring the cultivation of coffee and papaver flowers (opium poppy). The Sierra is a hot spot in the Colombian conflict, serving as home to the Caribbean Bloc of the FARC-EP and the Middle Magdalena Bloc of the FARC-EP, and an ELN guerrilla column, that have also strayed into Venezuelan territory.

In the early seventies, the Colombian authorities were reluctant to come on campaign and clarify the border with their Venezuelan counterparts.

Bari-Motilones

The head of the Venezuelan Frontiers Commission, Roman Rojas, decided to send a party to traverse the border and leave signs that the Colombian military might see when they flew over the area. Georges Pantchenko, the astronomer in charge of operations at the Comisión de Fronteras, asked me to go along as a rock-climber since it was anticipated that some parts might need a rope. Pantchenko had been in charge of the 1970 expedition to the headwaters of the Orinoco and was credited with having discovered the source of this mighty river. An astronomer was in charge because, once agreed, the frontier was marked by star readings, which were then embodied in an international treaty between the respective countries.

There is a delightful story about how, in 1957, Vera Loucach, George Panchenko's wife, ventured into the Amazonas region in search of her husband who she had disappeared. She asked a friend to fly her to Puerto Ayacucho from where she wanted to get a bongo to take her up river. People tried to persuade her it was futile and too dangerous, but she went anyway. A month after she'd heard about her husband's disappearance she embarked from Samariapo with her fiend, a member of the National Guard, a Brazilian and a Guahibo Indian who acted as pilot. She thought he might be at La Esmeralda on the Upper Orinoco. They stopped for fifteen days at San Fernando de Atabapo to repair the outboard. before continuing up river. They stopped at a Guaica (Yanomamo) village where Vera treated with mercurochrome a boy who had cut his hand. Sometime later Pantchenko came to the same place and, asked about the purple stain on the boy's hand. Hearing he had been treated by a blonde woman who was searching for her husband he realised it must have been Vera. He followed her up river and they were reunited near the Brazilian border at the headwaters of the Orinoco.

My boss, Manuel Corrao, was the Head of Urban Planning in the Venezuelan Ministerio de Obras Públicas. He called me into his office and informed me that I was being seconded to the Ministerio de Relaciones Exteriores for a couple of weeks.

The ridge we intended to walk was over 300 kilometres long, and the highest points are Cerro de Las Tetas at 3630 meters, followed by Cerro Irapa at 3540 meters. We flew by military helicopter from the town of Machiques to a base camp below the main ridge at about 3,000 metres.

We flew by military helicopter from Machiques to a base camp at 3,000m

The helicopter shook and juddered as it clawed its way up the side of the mountain, first over grassland, then dense forest, before the vegetation thinned to mountain paramo of low scrubs and coarse grasses.

We had a day and a night at base camp before setting of. Roman explained that the intended border determines our way. It is determined by the line of the watershed between the Maracaibo Basin in Venezuela and the Cesar-Ranchera Basin in Colombia. But the watershed, where the water that falls as rain either flows west into Colombia or east into Venezuela, is not that obvious. Where the ridge branches or changes direction, this line couldn't be determined on the available satellite images. Roman was a lovely clever man and I enjoyed talking to him and Jorge.

Roman had been the Ambassador to Guyana and was totally committed to determining Venezuela's borders with its neighbours, Guyana, Brazil and Colombia. The Essequibo, the part of Guyana west of the Essequibo river, was claimed by Venezuela. In 1835 the British government commissioned German-born explorer and naturalist Robert Hermann Schomburgk to survey British Guiana's boundaries. This survey resulted in what came to be known as the "Schomburgk Line". After a period of increasing tension the

Daniel Genoud, Román Rojas and Jorge Cardona

United States, representing Venezuela, entered into mediation with Britain, which resulted in the Paris Arbitration Award of 1899 which ceded the whole territory to Britain. Roman was determined to win it back.

Jorge Cardona was also interesting. His father Félix Cardona (1903-1982) was a famous Spanish explorer, cartographer, collector in Venezuela. Captain Félix Cardona was credited with being the first to climb Auyantepui, the immense table mountain, with Angel falls, the highest waterfall in the world, that was unknown to the outside world before 1930. Angel Falls is named after Jimmy Angel, the American aviator and soldier of fortune who crash landed on the summit in search of gold. There was a story. Angel claimed to have met an "old mining engineer" called McCracken in a bar in Panama, who hired him to fly to the summit of Auyántepui. Angel said that they landed near a summit stream, where in three days they collected 20 pounds of gold from the gravel in a stream. This was 1935, It's not clear if any of this was true. What was certain was that abundant gold and diamonds had been found in the Caroni River that flowed from Auyántepuy. Between 1935 and 1937 Jimmie and his wife Marie made several trips to Venezuela

El Rio Caroni, Jimmy Angel's plane, on the summit of Auyántepui

Gustavo Heny, a Venezuelan explorer, met Jimmie and Marie Angel in Ciudad Bolivar in 1937 and was intrigued by their plans. He agreed to help. Together with Felix Cardona and Miguel Delgado he began exploring a way up Auyántepuy's southern wall and found a cleft they could climb. Cardona returned to camp after a few days but Heny and Delgado continued but were barred from the northern end of the plateau, and Angel's proposed landing site, by a steep wall. They searched for gold but found none. On 9 October 1937, Jimmie, Marie, Henry and Miguel Delgado took off, leaving Cardona to man the radio back at base camp. Despite a perfect approach, the landing wheels broke through the crust and sank into the mud. Fortunately they were well prepared with food, ropes and tents. It took them 11 days to cross the plateau, descend the barrier wall and reach the trail Henry had found up the south wall. Angel's Flamingo plane, named *El Rio Caroni,* was rescued by the Venezuelan airforce and is on display at Ciudad Boliver Airport. The first scientific exploration, the Phelps Venezuelan Expedition of the American Museum of Natural History, made the first zoological and botanical collections the following year.

Angel Falls 979 meters

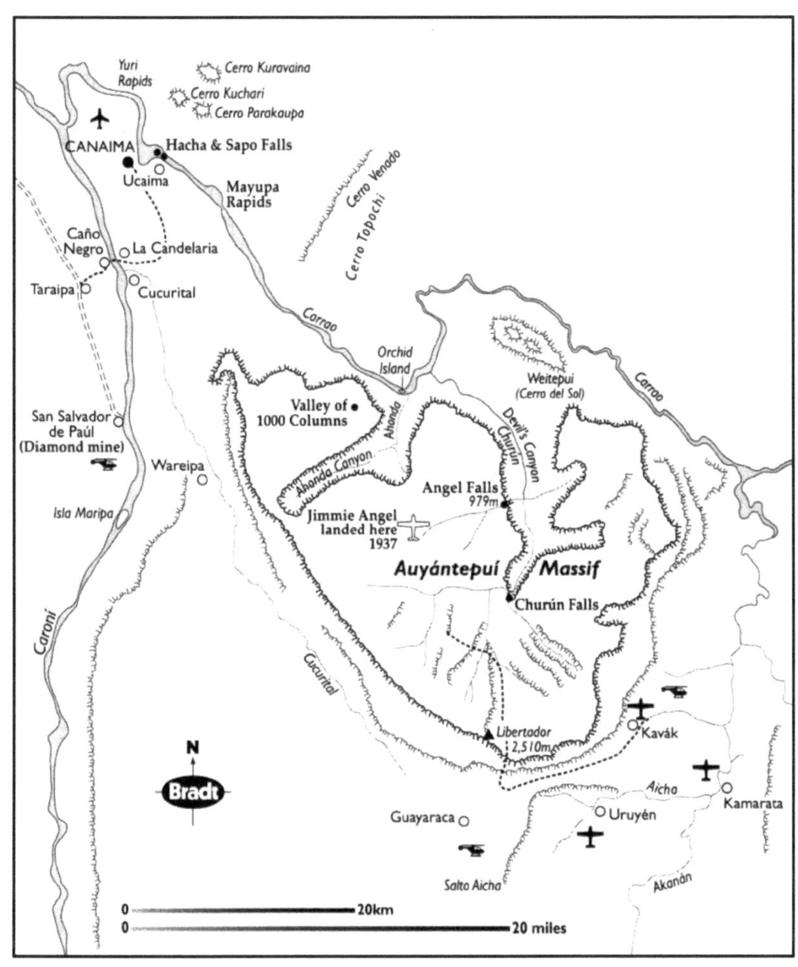

Auyántepui and Canaima

It took a couple of trips to ferry Daniel, me, four Makiritare Indians, and all our supplies to base camp. The Makiritare were from the Upper Ventuari River. Segundo was the leader, Tuco was older and Marco a young man. Our freeze-dried food was packed into large tins, one of which we used as a stock pot to cook over a wood fire. The Makiritare were equally at home here as in the Amazon.

Daniel decided the route and led the way. But he wasn't autocratic or over-bearing in any way. In the evening, before the light faded, he would discuss the next stage with Segundo and Marco and take their advice. And during the day they might gently suggest a better way. I just tagged along, relishing the freedom, the wild open terrain and enjoying the exercise. I accepted the principle of identifying the line of the watershed and following it, but the division wasn't always clear or why we might deviate from the obvious ridge line. Nevertheless things gradually made sense and when it was possible to look back a way and trace the day's march it was possible to see the whole route taking shape of an idea in the landscape, a dynamic version of the sense one gets in giving name to a peak or a river. The Makiritare made camp each night, found water where they seemed to be

Segundo carrying tent and shotgun. Marco and Tuco with food tins

none, cooked on an open fire and generally looked after us. They each had a machete and Daniel and I had film cameras, but apart from this, the tents, and the clothes on our backs, we carried little else.

Panchenko asked us to leave signs of our passing in the form of cairns that would be seen by the Colombian military. So we built 'hombrecitos', 'little men' stone pile sculptures on prominent or exposed tops, which would be seen from passing helicopters.

There was no sign of a path or a sign of anyone ever having been this way. Some parts involved scrambling up rocky outcrops or pushing through thick vegetation, typically where the way crossed a watercourse, but most progress was over open paramo, We would rise early and walk for eight or hours or so, covering as much as 30 kilometres a day. We walked for 6-7 days and each evening.

Daniel and I climbed all of the peaks we passed, leaving the Makiritare in camp. However, below Cerro Perijá, Daniel had a recurrence of malaria and had to spend the day in the tent and rest and recover. He had contracted a severe bout of malaria on an expedition on the Upper Orinoco. He had been home to Switzerland for treatment, but the disease

Daniel, Segundo and Marco

had returned. I was keen to climb. Daniel said there was no need. I said simply, I need to get to the top. It seemed important to complete our mission, but more pressingly it was there, a huge mass beckoning me upwards and I felt compelled to climb it. It was about Grade IV UIAA, hard enough soloing. A thick mist swirl about the cliffs, so I build cairns to help me find my way back. The climb was tiring and involved tricky scrambling but I felt elated and made it to the top and built a large cairn for the Colombians. Daniel was pleased to see me back safely.

It was a most successful and pleasurable trip. The Makiritare were unflaggingly cheerful and Daniel and I got on well. What was so amazing about this trip, and something I did not recognise at the time, is that in all likelihood no one had ever walked this frontier ridge. Indians, smugglers and guerrillas had crossed it in various places, but no one, I imagine, had ever walked along it, and I expect few have since.

At the end of the expedition we had arranged to be picked up by helicopter. We built a fire, and the pilot found us and flew us back to base camp.

Guiding the helicopter to our camp at the end of the expedition

Base camp

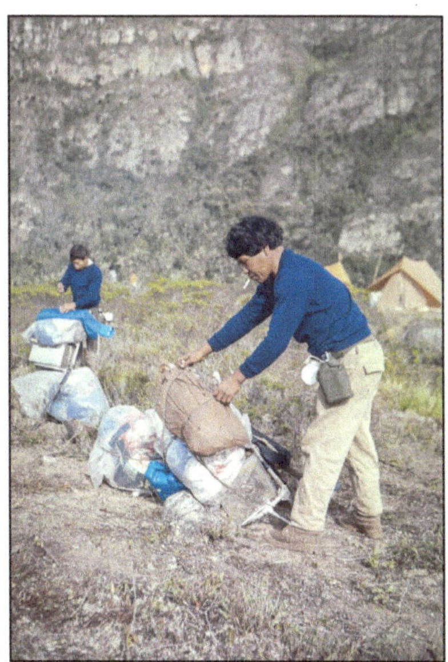

Packing loads at base camp

Scrambling up the ridge

Marco

Daniel

Segundo cooking dinner

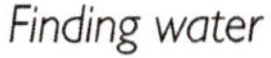

Finding water

Feeding an injured bird

Daniel eating dinner

Daniel

Climbing Cerro Perijá

Cerro Perijá

Climbing Cerro Perijá

Summit hombercito

Last camp

Border issues

Historical Background

The boundary dates back to the Spanish colonial division between the Captaincy General of Venezuela and the Viceroyalty of New Granada. The demarcation was vague, especially in the rugged Perijá mountains, leaving many valleys in dispute. After independence, the new republics of Venezuela and Colombia inherited these imprecise boundaries. Several agreements attempted to fix the border, notably the 1941 Treaty of Limits between Venezuela and Colombia, which formally defined most of the land border, including in the Perijá.

After the treaty several pockets of ambiguity remained over exact watershed lines in high mountain terrain, and disputes arose over access to natural resources or security concerns. The Perijá foothills contain significant coal deposits, especially in Zulia's Guasare and Socuy basins. In the 1970s, both legal and proposed mining projects in Venezuela and Colombia raised cross-border environmental and Indigenous rights concerns.

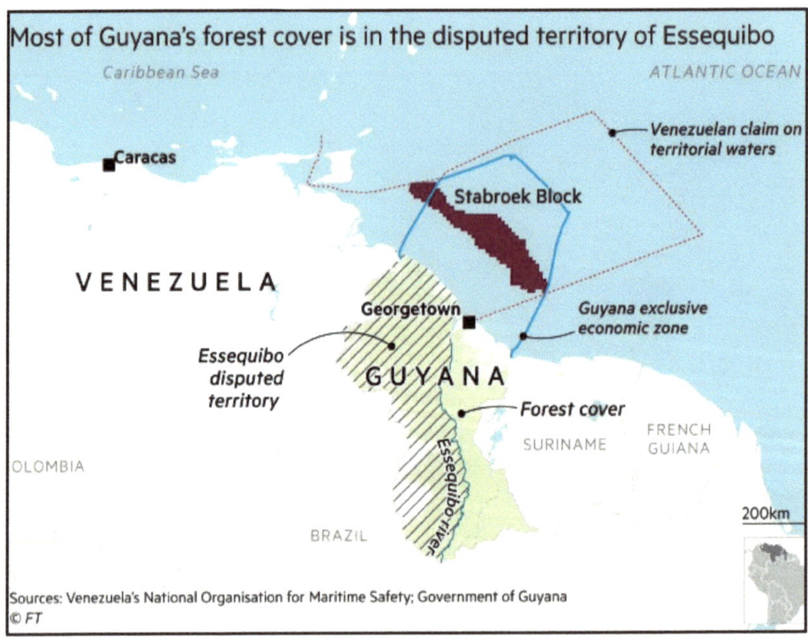

Essequibo, Zona en Reclamación claimed by Venezuela and issue of oil

Significance

The Sierra Perijá feeds key rivers flowing into Lake Maracaibo (Venezuela) and the Magdalena basin (Colombia). Control of watersheds has strategic importance for agriculture, hydropower potential, and urban supply. The lower slopes and valleys are fertile and contested between Indigenous land claims, settlers, and ranchers. The region's forests and páramos hold unique species and conservation policies sometimes conflict with economic projects and cross-border development plans.

Lake Maracaibo is the heart of Venezuela's oldest and most productive oil basin, including the Gulf of Maracaibo at its northern end. Many rivers originating in the Sierra de Perijá — such as the Socuy, Maché, and Palmar — drain eastward into Lake Maracaibo. These rivers supply freshwater that dilutes lake salinity, supports port operations, and maintains ecological balance in oil-producing zones.

Deforestation, mining, and cross-border conflict disrupt Perijá watersheds, and sedimentation and water quality in the lake could be affected, complicating oil infrastructure maintenance and navigation.

Pollution from oil wells in Lake Maracaibo

Security and Cross-Border Conflict

Since the late 20th century, Colombian armed groups (FARC, ELN) have used the Perijá range as a corridor for movement, recruitment, and illicit activities. The rugged, lightly monitored terrain facilitates smuggling and the movement of fuel, food, and contraband between the two countries. Indigenous communities often find themselves caught between armed actors, facing threats, displacement, and recruitment pressures.

Frontier Commissions and Demarcation

Venezuela and Colombia established commissions to survey and mark boundary lines, including mountain sectors in Perijá. In the 1970s, these were sometimes linked to exploratory expeditions to map valleys and peaks. However, the rough terrain, limited access, and political tensions often slowed field demarcation. In many Indigenous areas, formal border markers have less meaning than traditional territorial boundaries.

Ongoing Issues

Mining (especially coal) remain controversial due to their environmental impact, Indigenous opposition, and potential to exacerbate cross-border

Paso Diablo coal mine Guasare

disputes. Venezuela's Sierra de Perijá National Park (established 1978) protects part of the range, but enforcement is uneven, and activities on the Colombian side can still affect ecosystems. Both countries face internal debates about recognising Indigenous territories, which often span the border, challenging the Westphalian notion of hard boundaries.

The Sierra de Perijá's border issues are a mix of historic demarcation disputes, strategic resource competition, and security challenges, over laying a culturally and ecologically sensitive landscape. Maintaining clear control of the Perijá border strengthens Venezuela's overall claim to the Zulia oil basin, which is geographically close to Colombia and historically contested in small ways (especially in pre-1941 negotiations). Roman Rojas and his team were concerned that a weak presence along the Perijá frontier could embolden illegal economic activity or undermine perceptions of Venezuelan control in Zulia and the Maracaibo basin oil.

Timeline

Pre-Colonial Era – Before 1500s

The Sierra is inhabited by Indigenous groups, notably the Yukpa on the eastern slopes and the Barí on the west. Their territories cross what is now the Venezuela–Colombia border, with seasonal and trade movements between valleys. *Colonial Period – 1500s–1810*

The area falls within the Spanish Empire, split between the Captaincy General of Venezuela and the Viceroyalty of New Granada. The division is vague, with no precise demarcation in the mountainous Perijá sector. Missionary settlements and small military outposts are established on both sides, competing for Indigenous converts and trade routes.

Post-Independence – Early 1800s

Venezuela and Colombia emerge from the collapse of Gran Colombia. The old colonial administrative line is used as a reference, but remains unmarked in much of the Sierra. Sporadic disputes arise over ranching lands and Indigenous territory, but the range remains largely un-surveyed.

1930s – Frontier Survey Missions

Joint expeditions (Comisión de Fronteras Colombo-Venezolana) begin to survey the northern Andes sectors, including the headwaters of the Río de Oro in Barí territory. Early aerial reconnaissance and topographic mapping improved knowledge of Perijá's ridges and passes.

1941 – Treaty of Limits

Venezuela and Colombia sign a formal border treaty, settling most boundary disputes. In the Sierra de Perijá sector the watershed line forms the legal boundary. Despite this, ground demarcation is incomplete.

1960s – Resource Interest Grows

Geological surveys on the Venezuelan side reveal large coal deposits in the foothills of Perijá, especially in Zulia's Guasare and Socuy basins. Mining raises questions about environmental impact and Indigenous displacement.

1970s – Frontier Commission & State-Supported Exploration

Venezuela's Frontier Commission and military logistics support scientific and exploratory expeditions in Perijá, including mapping and speleology around Cerro Pintado. Border marking continues in accessible passes, but dense forests and security risks slow progress.

1980s – Escalation of Security Issues

Colombian guerrilla groups (FARC, ELN) use Perijá as a corridor for movement and refuge. Armed encounters occur along the border, affecting Indigenous and settler communities. Smuggling routes for goods, fuel, and cattle develop, often crossing Indigenous lands.

1990s – Mining and Indigenous Land Claims

Venezuelan coal projects expand in Zulia, prompting Yukpa protests over land rights and environmental damage. On the Colombian side, small-scale mining and deforestation increase in lower slopes of Perijá.

2000s – Intensified Conflict and Displacement

Violence between armed groups and the Colombian military pushes civilians (including Barí) toward the Venezuelan side. Yukpa leaders demand formal demarcation of Indigenous territories.

2008–2015 – High-Profile Land Rights Struggles

Yukpa land rights conflicts in Venezuela lead to confrontations with ranchers, police, and the military. Some Yukpa territories are officially titled, but disputes over boundaries and land use persist.

2010s – Environmental vs. Development Tensions

Proposals to reopen or expand coal mining in Perijá reignite debates about cross-border environmental impact. Illegal logging, fires, and agricultural expansion continue to erode forest cover in both countries.

Present Day

The legal border is fixed, but enforcement is uneven due to the rugged terrain and limited state presence. Security, environmental conservation, and resource extraction continue to define the political and economic stakes in the Sierra de Perijá.

Potential Future Development

There have been exploratory studies in western Zulia suggesting oil and gas potential in foothill and sub-Andean zones near Perijá. However, any expansion of oil extraction would place making security, cross-border diplomacy, and Indigenous land rights even more difficult.

People crossing the border

Indigenous peoples

Motilone (Bari and Yukpa)

Two indigenous groups, the Bari and the Yukpa peoples, inhabit the Sierra Perijá. The Yukpa live on the Venezuelan side of the border in the northern section of the ridge Daniel and I traversed. The Bari live further south on either side of the ridge in both Venezuela and Colombia in the section Daniel and Wilmur traversed.

Both are commonly referred to as "Motilones", which means "shaved heads" in Spanish. But this is not how they refer to themselves. They are descendants of the Tairona culture concentrated in northeastern Colombia and western Venezuela. Both groups are bi-national and frequently cross the border. In recent years, a significant number of people from both groups have migrated from Venezuela to Colombia due to the economic and humanitarian crisis in Venezuela. This migration complicates accurate population estimation.

Indigenous groups in Venezuela

Bari

The total population of Bari is uncertain, and different sources have it as low as 5400 in Colombia and 1000 in Venezuela and as high as 11,000. The Barí people have historically faced significant population decline due to massacres, disease, and displacement caused by conflicts and oil and gas exploitation. However, the establishment of reserves has helped stabilise and promote population growth.

Each group is composed of about 50 people, who have up to three malokas (communal houses), each of which houses several nuclear families. They settle for about ten years in a site near rivers abundant in fish. At the centre of the maloka are the hearths, and along the sides the sleeping areas of each family. Marriages are arranged between allies and prohibited between relatives. In the maloka, each family is placed so that neighbours are the man's allies and the woman's relatives.

Like many other indigenous people in Venezuela, the Barí are farmers, hunters, fishers, and gatherers. Around their communal houses, they cultivate cassava, sweet potato, plantain, squash, corn, yams, pineapple, sugarcane, cocoa, cotton, annatto, and chilli peppers. They use bows and

Bari people

arrows for hunting and fishing, and hunt birds, monkeys, peccaries, tapirs, and rodents. Fishing is an important food source, and to increase it, they build temporary dams and use barbasco (a fish poison). They have traded since time immemorial to obtain salt, and, nowadays, for metal tools, radios, batteries, and other items.

Bari fishing

Yukpa

The total population of Yukpa is estimated to be 9,400 in Venezuela and 1,900 in Colombia. The Yukpa face numerous challenges, including displacement and loss of their ancestral lands due to armed conflict, deforestation, mining projects, and the expansion of cattle ranching. Children in particular suffer from high rates of malnutrition and inadequate access to schooling.

Yukpa ancestral lands encompass areas with diverse ecosystems, including mountains and tropical rainforests. They were first contacted in the 16th century, and the Spanish conquered and forced them to convert to Christianity. Their population was decimated by disease and forced labour, and they had to abandon their traditional culture and way of life. They have only survived because the rugged terrain helped preserve their culture and way of life. They have a rich and elaborate history and were known for their hunting and fishing, as well as their knowledge of local plants and animals. The Yukpa had a complex system of social and political organisation.

In the last fifty years, Yukpa settlement patterns have changed radically in

Yukpa people

response to economic pressures and the influence of Capuchin missionaries. Yukpa communities have moved closer to the plains adjoining the mountain and to local towns adjacent to mission stations. Many Yukpa now work on large dairy ranches, where they spend weeks before returning to their families in the mountains.

History

In 1499, an expedition led by Alonso de Ojeda visited the Venezuelan coast and discovered the Maracaibo Basin. The stilt houses in the area of Lake Maracaibo reminded the Italian navigator, Amerigo Vespucci, of the city of Venice, Italy, so he named the region Veneziola, or "Little Venice". The Spanish version of Veneziola is Venezuela.

The Spaniards believed that the area's frequent lightning strikes turned stone into gold, and so they began settling the region extensively. The Motilones fought the Spaniards back from their territory, defeating five royal expeditions sent to pacify the Indians.

In 1530, Ambrosius Ehinger, commissioned by the banking family, Welser of Augsburg, looted a large amount of gold from the Kalina people on the

Alonso de Ojeda landing in La Guajira

western coast of South America and attempted to transport the gold over the Bobalí Mountains. Bari Indians ambushed and destroyed the expedition, and the gold was lost, never to be found again. Motilon warriors also harassed the troops of Simón Bolívar in the 19th century as he led them over the Andes Mountains into the Orinoco plain. This cemented their reputation as a fierce people.

Bari resistance was particularly intense between 1530 and 1730. Capuchin missionaries studied their language, began to catechise some groups, and formed Indigenous settlements. At first, these settlements were attacked by the Barí, just as Spanish ones were. Still, beginning in 1772, the government of Maracaibo managed to establish peaceful contact that eventually included at least 21 Barí communities.

In 1905, the government of General Rafael Reyes granted General Virgilio Barco a concession to exploit oil, coal, and asphalt in Barí territory. Oil was discovered, and as oil companies moved in, Bari land was drilled for oil from 1913 to 1926. By the late 1920s, the Barí were at war. Exploitation began in earnest again from 1996 to 2001.

Palafitos in Lake Maracaibo

Since the initial contact in 1650, Bari land has been reduced to 7% of its original extent, and the Bari have shifted their production to the gardening of cash crops to acquire Western goods, which are becoming increasingly integrated into their culture. Their chief economic activity is the growing of Theobroma cacao, the plant from which chocolate is made. They export the cacao and use the proceeds to help maintain their network of schools, community centres, and health clinics.

Makiritare (Yekuana)

The Makiritare are are a Caribe-speaking tropical rainforest tribe. They are also known as Yekuana or boat people because of their fame in building the large dug-out canoes, bongos and curiaras, that are the workhorse craft of the Orinoco. They refer to themselves as So'to or "people". Their home is on the Caura River and Upper Ventuari River regions of Venezuela. They live in circular communal houses called atta. According to the Census, there were about 6,000 Makiritare living in Venezuela in 2001. In Brazil, they inhabit the northeast of Roraima State. In Venezuela, the Ye'kuana live alongside their former enemies, the Yanomami.

Makiritare constructing a curiara dug-out

ORINOCO 1973

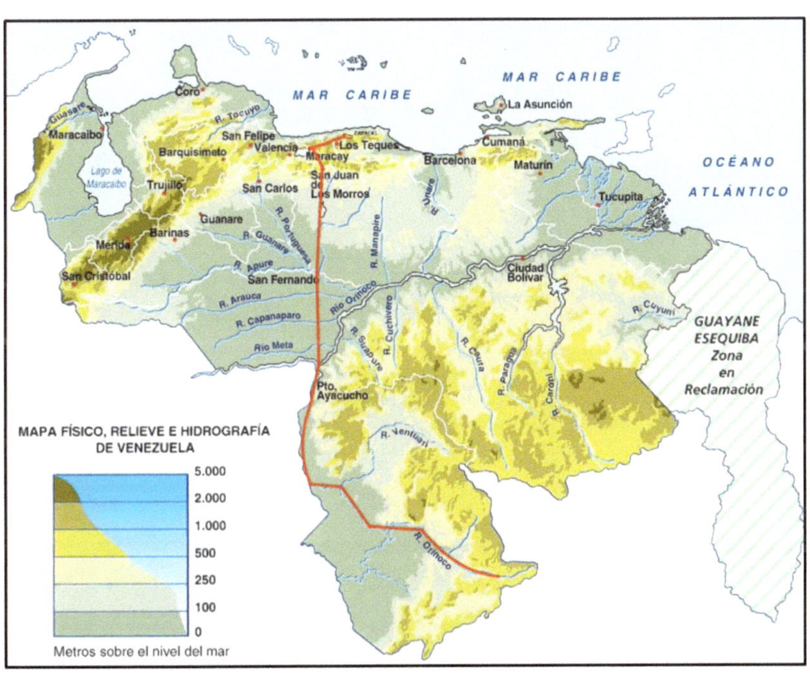

Route across the Llanos and up the Orinoco

I got a call from Daniel Genoud, my friend in the Frontiers Commission, asking if I was free to go on a trip up the Orinoco to rescue Jacques Lizot. Jacques was a French anthropologist who had been living with the Yanomami in a teri or settlement on the Upper Orinoco. Jacques had managed to get a message to Daniel that the Silesian missionaries at Esmeralda disapproved of him, had stolen his clothes and were withholding his mail and supplies. Nothing was said about why.

A friend, Wilmer Perez, would be coming. Wilmer had a Toyota Jeep, and I had a long-wheelbase Land Rover. The idea was to drive to Puerto Ayacucho on the Orinoco, and from there take a bongo upriver. A bongo is a large dugout canoe. Daniel wouldn't be able to come with us because he had something else to do. We could hire a bongo in Samariapo, but we needed to take two outboard motors, an inflatable boat and food.

Wilmer and I loaded the gear and set off together with a friend. The first bit, to Calabozo, was on paved roads, but from there it was dirt tracks across the bare llanos. From Caracas, we drove west to Villa de Cura and past San Juan de los Moros – four hundred and thirty-seven kilometres in five hours. This part was familiar, but after Calabozo, everything was new

Venezuelan Royal Palm (Roystonea oleracea)

Rio Capanaparo

and exciting. Today, the road is the Troncal 2 and is paved for much of the way. Not so in 1972.

We crossed the great Apure River at nine-thirty and left the hard top soon after. From the San Fernando de Apure to the Orinoco it was only two hundred and twenty kilometres. I'd measured it. But there were no roads shown on the map I'd managed to get, nor any bridges across the nine rivers. The broad dirt track soon petered out. At times, the track almost disappeared. It was hot and sweaty, and there were sand flies at the rivers. They didn't bother me that much, but one man working the ferry, bare-chested, was covered in red bites.

Wilmer, in his Toyota Land Cruiser, charged ahead, while I followed in my Land Rover. The plain, green now after the rains, stretched flat in all directions. We were the first to cross this season. There were intermittent traces of old tracks but Wilmer seemed to navigate by instinct, using the sketchy directions we got at the occasional habitations at river crossings. The flatness of the plain was relieved only by palms – three in a clump, then four in a line, like beacons in a grass sea. We came to small

Dirt track at first, then faint tire tracks or nothing

Men under a mango tree

Life in the Llanos

settlements with houses of mud and thatched roofs. Men at rustic tables chatting and playing cards in the shade of spreading mango trees. A young boy in a straw hat pushing a barrow with four tin cans full of water from the well. And in the wide open plains, llanero 'cowboys' on stringy horses rounding cattle with bare toes in steel stirrups. We drove until dark and camped under the stars, slung in hammocks between the two vehicles. It was magical, sleeping under the stars and gazing up at the black canopy of the sky.

The Land Rover was older than the Toyota but seemed to manage the swamps better. We'd bought it with the idea of travelling through South America with the children. I'd even contacted a literary agent, John Farquharson, about the project. He'd been encouraging us to try writing about the trip from our different viewpoints. Our previous car, A Wiley's Jeep that we had bought with my first paycheck after we'd been without money for six months, was totalled by a friend while we were on a visit to England. I'd fitted out the Land Rover as a simple camper-van and we'd travelled all over Venezuela in it, including the Guajira, Coro, Merida and the Gran Sabana.

Unloading petrol tank from Wilmer's Toyota

Toyota Land Cruiser and Wilmer unloading outboard motor

We hit the first swamp about noon. Wilmer came to a sudden dead halt and sank to the axles. There had been nothing to distinguish this puddle from dozens of others we'd splashed through. The Toyota gently listed to one side, water now well above the door sill. Wilmer climbed out. "Good that you put your climbing rope in," he said. "It will ruin it," I said. "What else are we going to do?" I braided the long rope into a stout hawser while Wilmer unloaded the roof rack of petrol tanks and an outboard motor. There were no gas stations until Puerto Ayacucho, so we carried jerry cans and a large petrol tank. I got good at siphoning the petrol without swallowing too much.The tow rope stretched alarmingly until, the jeep popped out with a loud sucking sound, like a tight cork out of a bottle. We followed this pattern for the rest of the day and most of the following. The rope finally gave out, chewed and frayed. We were stuck. Wilmer walked half a mile to a solitary palm and cut it down with my machete. We inserted the ten-foot length under the rear axle of the jeep and levered it out of the quagmire.

Halfway across, on the morning of the second day, we came upon a man on horse-back. His name was Simon Bolivar, named after the Libertador. His family had lived there for five generations. He sat easily on the horse, the toes of his bare feet stuck through metal stirrups. The horse was lean, almost emaciated. The man rode ahead of us, leading the way to his home. The horse covered the ground in long, easy strides; it looked as though it could keep going forever. His house was made of red mud on wattle with a tin roof, large for a man and a woman living alone. There was a dirt yard enclosed by a pole fence and shaded by a spreading rain-tree. The man dismounted and invited us to stop and eat.

Wilmer rode the man's horse while the man's wife cooked. Wilmer galloped like he drove, with wild abandon. I sat in the shade under a spreading mango tree. There was a stone urn in the crook of a pale trunk under a pomelo tree heavty with fruit. It looked as though it had been there for centuries; perhaps it had. Every few minutes, there was a soft plop as a drop of water, like a bright jewel, detached itself from the smooth underside of the stone and fell into a calabash below. I dipped the ladle into the water and drank. It was deliciously cool. We ate outside under the mango at the back of the house. Through the open door, I

Llanero cowboy

could see inside the house. There was a hide chair, greasy from long use, and a rickety table. A hammock stretched between the stout cross beams was their bed. Another, perhaps for visitors, hung in a ball. A notched spar led into the darkness of a loft, maybe used for storing valuables. Most likely, they had few possessions other than the three saddles on the hitching rail and perhaps a trunk containing best clothes for going to town.

The meal was scrambled eggs, pork and beans. The man's wife wouldn't sit with us, but stood nearby, smiling. She was younger than the man, and looked Indian. She had lost her front teeth, but was beautiful nevertheless. The man talked with Wilmer about the land, about cattle and the drought last year. Too soon we had to leave, roaring away in a cloud of dust, leaving me wondering what it would be like to live in such isolation, such simplicity.

Late in the afternoon, we reached a track through woodland and knew we must be reaching the Orinoco. It had taken over twenty hours to reach Puerto Paez. It was late afternoon. I had imagined a quay, but there was nothing but the river, the forest and the smooth black rocks as old as time. We parked the jeeps one behind the other on black slabs sloping down to the muddy river. And we lay on the warm rock in the evening light and waited for a ferry. The river was half a mile wide.

Already the journey was like a series of snap- shots, river crossings merging into one another, losing the regular order suggested by my note-book: Apure, Payara, Apurito, Cunaviche, Capanaparo, Cano Manteco and Cinaruco,twice. Now the Orinoco. A meaningless litany of names. Only isolated incidents and dislocated faces remained, like oases in featureless space. Memories pinned to my cortex by the snapping of my camera. A vision of white sheets laid on pebbles to dry, suddenly lifting high into the air and floating away over the trees. Women screaming and disappearing after them along forest tracks. My sketch map told me nothing. A dotted line, punctuated by mud-holes and swamps. Driving was no way to travel, no way to enter into the landscape. It would be better to ride or walk. Everything seems impossibly hard when you drive. We could have walked it in less than a week, taking it easy, stopping to look and talk. The silent dialogue wouldn't stop. How do you see new things if you have no name for them? There was a whole world back there, the way we had come, as complex and as fascinating as any world I knew, but I hadn't seen it. My view had been blinkered by our objective, getting to the Orinoco.

Wilmer waved. He had been exploring along the bank, and now flopped down at my side. "No sign of a boat yet. The Meta joins a mile upstream. It's bringing all the mud that's making the river so brown. Colombia is on the other side. Daniel and I were on campaign with the Colombians last year, on the Arauca. It's so flat, the rivers just wind around. We packed it in when they started using explosives to divert the flow. It is so much easier with the Brazilians. They're all military, of course, but so professional and great fun."

"What happens now?" I asked. "We wait", said Wilmur. "Talking about fun, I thought I'd die laughing on the Payara crossing. The guy on the bank shouted caribe (piranha) and you came out of the water like a jack-in-the-box!" "I heard him as I was diving. I don't think I even got wet!"

In the distance, we saw a strange craft. As it drew near, we could see it was a catamaran formed from two dug-out canoes; a ramshackled two-storey structure with a green plastic window on the upper deck, illuminated by the setting sun. A old man waved and then gently ran the craft aground on a partly submerged rock. He lowered two planks. They formed a steep ramp, and there was just enough room on the chalana for the jeep in the fenced enclosure straddling the canoes.

Wilmer insisted I go first. Unable to see the deck of the chalana because of the steep incline, I drove slowly, in the lowest gear, imagining overshooting and tumbling into the river on the other side. I climbed out of the vehicle and watched as the old man put the outboard in gear and thrust off the bank with a long pole. Out on the river, there was a light breeze, and the water was choppy. The tiller set, the craft steered itself while the man busied himself pumping out the dug-outs. I imagined that the fenced enclosure must be used for transporting cattle, as I stepped carefully to avoid the signs of recent occupancy. Above the stern, the man had his home – an open room, screened by plastic, with a hammock, aluminium cooking pots and a large calabash for drinking water.

Chalana Orinoco ferry to Puerto Ordaz

Wilmur followed and then we drove in convoy along a road beside the river south to Pueblo Ayacucho, the capital. The next day, we drove 70 kilometres to Samariapo and spent much of the day kicking our heels and getting organised. Boats going upriver start from here to avoid the Atures rapids. We had now acquired two more friends of Daniel, a couple. He was a Swiss filmmaker and came along for the ride.

We set off with a couple of Makiritare, one at the tiller and the other in the bow, keeping a lookout for rocks. We were loaded with two oil drums of gasoline for the outboard motors. Travelling by dugout on the Orinoco

Loaded curiara crossing Orinoco

Makiritare in bow of bongo

Wilmer and Swiss on roof of the bongo

is a delightfully lazy form of travel. We sat on the roof of the boat and watched the world go by. Other river craft, white egrets in the trees and the dense green wall of the forest. The beat of the engines and the boat creaming through the water is hypnotic, and at night we slept in hammocks slung under the cabin roof. Wilmer inflated the rubber boat we'd brought with us and attached the spare outboard, and we went water skiing with bare feet.

We passed San Fernando de Atabapo and Santa Barbara, where the Rio Ventuari joins the Orinoco. The water is like warm milk, cloudy with sediment and nutrients. But where the Brazo Casiquiare joins the Orinoco the confluence is a stunning, hard line between the black and brown streams. The Casiquiare is a tributary of the Orinoco that forms a canal between the Orinoco and Amazon river systems. This is stream capture in action, and although the volume of water captured from the Orinoco is relatively small, eventually the Cunacunuma River will be diverted to the Amazon.

When I felt thirsty, I could tip my tin mug over the side and scoop up a full mug of water. And when we stopped, we could slip over the side and

Marahuaca 2,832 m

cool off. We passed the imposing Cerro Duida and Cerro Marahuaka. This table mountain is an important cultural site for Yanomami and the home of tapir and harpy eagle. It can be climbed from Esmeralda, which we passed after Tamatama, but that wasn't part of the plan. Although I'd much like to stop and climb it, we don't have time.

We pass Santa Maria de Los Guaicas and reach the confluence of the Rio Mavaca. From here the Orinoco narrows. It's getting late, and we are racing along passed Platanal, trying to reach Jacque's village before nightfall. We had switched boats in La Esmeralda and are now in a smaller dugout without a roof called a curiara. We are going as fast as the huge outboard motor will take us when we strike a submerged rock. The boy in the bow has been avoiding the rocks till now by giving hand signals to the pilot at the tiller, but this rock has evaded him, and we come to a juddering halt. We are in rapids, and the water is boiling around us. It is a dark night and the stars are out. We could hardly hear each other shout over the roar of the waves. We slip into the water and start to heave the heavy log off the rock. It's hard work, and I feel my shoulder muscles straining, but eventually we lever it off and get going again. It's late, and we don't go far. Our pilot

One family's nano or section of the communal round-house

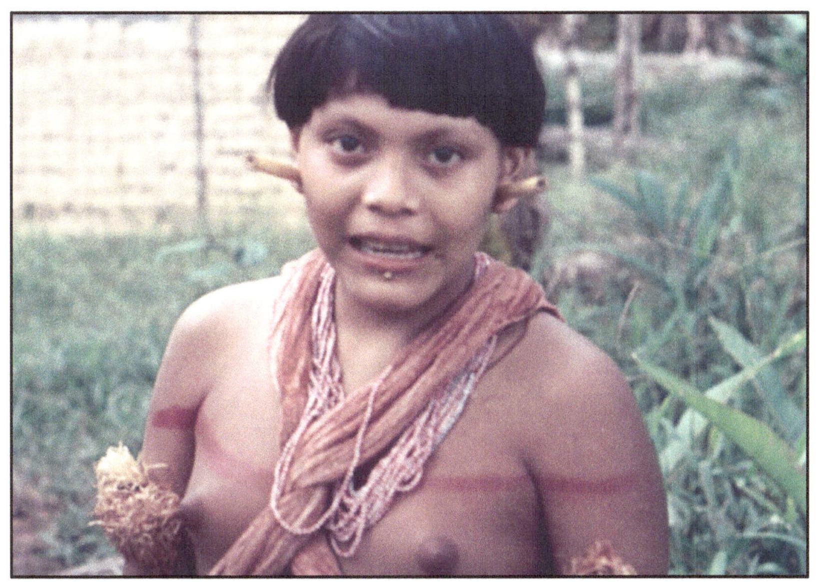

Young girl in Jaques Lizot's village

Helping construct new shabono

has decided to stop at the next settlement, a small Yanomami teri by the side of the river. The Indians are alarmed by our arrival in the dark, fearing the worst, but they welcome us in. I sling my hammock by feel under the thatch roof. There are swarms of mosquitoes, and remembering Daniel's malaria, I crawl into my sleeping bag. It's hot for a down bag, but I don't want to get bitten, and the bag is old and thin. It's my orange sleeping bag from scouts that I've had since I was 12. It gets impregnated by the wood smoke from the fire.

In the early morning, we reach Jacque's village and Wilmer and the others seem to disappear. I don't know where they've gone or what the plan is. So I wander around the settlement. Two women approach me.

Yanomami man bailing out his curiara

One has a baby on her arm. The other is a young girl with bare breasts. She comes close and feels my chest. I'm not sure what she wants. I suspect she's offering herself. She finds a comb in the pocket of my khaki shirt. I'm not sure why it's there, since I rarely comb my hair. She takes it out and indicates she wants it. They lose interest in me, and I wander on through the vegetable gardens. They are growing maize, squash and beans. The track leads a few hundred meters to a shabono, or communal house, that is under construction. It seems that after a while, the thatch deteriorates, the area becomes filthy, and the community builds a new house and relocates. A man is sitting on one of the main cross beams. He gestures for me to pass him a spar from a pile of timber. So I work away for a couple of hours, handing up building materials.

Jacques is finally ready to leave. His little hut is most Spartan – just a hammock, a simple desk, and little else. The journey back takes a couple of days but seems quicker than the journey out. Jacques is taciturn. Perhaps his is sad to be leaving or maybe it's uncertainty about the future prospects of getting back. So the return trip doesn't seem as much fun as when we were on an adventure to rescue Jacques. His precious research notes are

Jacques in the bow on the return journey

in a yellow oilskin bag but he has little else.

When we get back to Samariapo, there is a problem with the Land Rover. It lacks power. We find a garage in Puerto Ayacucho, and it seems that a rubber diaphragm in the injection pump has split. They haven't got a replacement, and there doesn't seem to be a solution, until someone suggests cutting a patch off the inflatable boat cover. Amazingly, the mechanic fashions a new diaphragm, and we're able to set off.

At the Cinaruco, instead of using the oil drum raft, I judge it to be shallow enough to risk driving through. Halfway across I climb out to take a photograph of the vehicle in the water and nearly step on an Amazonian stingray. I'm barefoot, and it would have given me a painful wound from its venomous spines. Luckily, it swam off. Unfortunately, on a second river crossing, climbing out of the river up a steep bank, the spare tire snags on the ground and rips off the back door of the Land Rover. I was annoyed, not least because from then on, the vehicle filled with dust, which covered everything in a film of dirt. Perhaps because of this, or maybe because I didn't hit it off with Jacques who seemed most taciturn, I didn't enjoy the journey home.

Rio Cinaruco

River crossing

Jacques has been living with the Yanomami a long while. He was vitriolic about the missionaries and about his rival anthropologist, Napoleon Chagnon. Being away from everyday life and civilisation had affected him profoundly, and social isolation has made him irritable and hypersensitive. In Puerto Ayacucho, he was mistrustful and even paranoid. At one point, when we were walking together down the Avenida Orinoco, we ran into the bishop, a lovely elderly man with a white beard like Father Christmas in a white soutane with a pith helmet. I liked him, so I stopped to chat. Jacque was horrified and attempted to hide behind a fire hydrant by the side of the road. The bishop just ignored this odd behaviour and chatted.

Later, after we had reached Caracas, Daniel organised a dinner at a restaurant to welcome Jacques back. He arrived naked to the waist, and when the waiter brought the food, he upturned the table and threw the food against the wall, railing against the trappings of civilisation, social convention and the artificiality of city life. It could have been embarrassing, but I found it compelling and enjoyed the show, though it left me hungry when we were thrown out. That was the last time I saw Jacques. He went back to France and died in 2022, aged 84, in Saleh, Morocco.

Anthropology

I studied anthropology for my first degree at Manchester University, and although much of the ethnographic material taught was based in Africa, one teacher lecturing about life in South American barrios caught my attention and influenced my decision to move to Venezuela in 1970. Working for the Frontiers Commission and exploring the interior brought me into contact with various indigenous groups, including the Yanomami people of the Venezuelan Amazon.

Some years ago I watched a TV programme about an academic scandal involving two anthropologists, Napoleon Chagnon, from MIT and Jacques Lizot from the Levi Strauss Institute in Paris. They both lived with Yanomami in the Upper Orinoco for some years beginning in the late 1960s. The programme accused Lizot of sexual exploitation and paedophilia and Chagnon of exposing people to measles as part of an experiment funded by the US Atomic Energy Commission. I met both men, talked to them about their work and, as related earlier, had spent a few days with Jacques in a dug-out canoe. So I had more than a passing

Jacques Lizot and Yanomami informants

interest in these revelations.

As well as describing the scandalous conduct of these two anthropologists the programme also suggested that their research was suspect; that they had been biased in their focus Chagnon, the American, had focused on the competition for scarce resources and had over emphasised warfare in the lives of Yanomamo and Lizot had focused on language and had thirty different words for penis stroking.

Jacques Lizot

Jacques Lizot, a French anthropologist and linguist, spent over two decades among the Yanomami, beginning in the late 1960s. His focus was on documenting the cultural complexity of Yanomami society. Works such as The Yanomami in the Face of Ethnocide (1976) and Tales of the Yanomami (1985)presented the group not as primitive or violent, but as a people with a rich cosmology, intricate kinship systems, and creative oral traditions. Lizot also sought to defend them against encroachment by miners, missionaries, and developers.

Yet Lizot was not free from controversy. Allegations emerged that he

Napoleon Chagnon

engaged in exploitative sexual relations with young Yanomami men. These claims, which circulated in anthropological circles and surfaced during the Darkness in El Dorado debate in 2000, cast a shadow over his reputation. While some colleagues defended his scholarship, critics argued that his personal conduct blurred ethical boundaries and damaged trust with his subjects. Unlike Chagnon, Lizot was not accused of manipulating data, but rather of failing the ethical responsibilities of an anthropological fieldworker.

Napoleon Chagnon

Napoleon Chagnon, an American anthropologist, first visited the Yanomami in 1964 as a graduate student. His book Yanomamö: The Fierce People (1968) became one of the most widely read ethnographies in anthropology, selling hundreds of thousands of copies. This book deeply influenced my own attitude to Yanomami. Chagnon's portrayal was stark: the Yanomami were described as living in a state of chronic warfare, with male aggression central to their culture. He argued that reproductive success among Yanomami men correlated with acts of killing, presenting this as an example of sociobiological evolution in action.

His methods were pioneering, and his findings fuelled the rise of

Jaques Lizot and Napoleon Chagnon

evolutionary anthropology. However, his depiction of the Yanomami as "the fierce people" drew criticism. Many anthropologists argued that he exaggerated violence, ignoring other aspects of Yanomami life. People claimed that his work reinforced harmful stereotypes that justified state neglect or even justified military and extractive incursions.

Yanomami

The Yanomami are an Arawak speaking people living in the highlands of the Upper Orinoco and northern Brazil. They are one of the most successful groups in the Amazon rainforest, living in harmony with their environment. They are believed to be the most primitive, culturally intact people in the world. They are literally a Stone Age tribe. They have never discovered the wheel, and the only metal they use is what has been traded to them from the outside. Their numbering system is one, two, and more than two. They cremate their dead, then crush and drink their bones in a final ceremony intended to keep their loved ones with them forever. They are hunters and gatherers who also tend small garden plots. Like so many other indigenous populations, the Yanomami have suffered through contact with 'white' men.

Yanomami archer

There are about 200 to 350 Yanomami villages scattered widely throughout their territory, each supporting between 40 and 150 people. In most villages, people build a single communal hut, about 100 feet wide, called a shabono. In the middle is an open plaza where children play and adults perform rituals. Each family builds its own section of the shabono, called a nano, which features an open fire.

The Yanomami rely on a primitive agricultural technique called "slash and burn." Forests and woodlands are cut and burned to create fields. The women weave and decorate the baskets. Baskets are fashioned from palm fibres and decorated to make both flat baskets and burden baskets, which are carried by a strap around the forehead.

The Yanomami, as well as other Indian tribes in the Amazon Basin, hunt with blow guns or bows and arrows.

For the blowguns, a piece of cane is used to fashion the shaft, and the darts are made from sharpened fibres and balanced on the end with cotton or the fibre of the kapok tree. They use poison from the poison dart frog to dip the ends of the darts in. For the bows and arrows, a flexible piece of wood fashions the bow and is strung with a hand-spun

Shabono or communal hut

fibre. The arrows are fletched with feathers and each has a different type of arrowhead carved from hardwood designed to hunt different sizes of game – birds, small mammals and larger mammals.

The Yanomami smoke a hallucinogenic drug called yopo. Yopo is made by grinding several natural roots and vines that are gathered in the rainforest. Smoking the drug is very painful, causing blinding pain in the head and nausea. After achieving a trance state, they communicate with the spirit world, relating their visions through chanting and dancing.

Controversy

The long-standing disputes surrounding Chagnon's work erupted with Patrick Tierney's book *Darkness in El Dorado* (2000), which accused him (and geneticist James Neel) of serious ethical violations. Tierney alleged that Chagnon manipulated conflicts, distributed steel tools to exacerbate tensions, and facilitated medical experiments during a measles epidemic. Although many of Tierney's charges were later discredited, the controversy damaged Chagnon's reputation and exposed deep divisions in anthropology.

Yanomami warriors

Chagnon and Lizot offered different pictures of Yanomami life. For Chagnon, violence and evolutionary logic explained social structures. For Lizot, myth, ritual, and cultural resilience were paramount. Their rivalry was both academic and ideological, and both anthropologists became symbols in larger battles within the discipline. Chagnon's defenders praised his rigorous data collection and evolutionary insights, while critics charged that his emphasis on violence distorted reality and fuelled stereotypes. Lizot was lauded for his deep immersion and cultural sensitivity, but his alleged misconduct raised questions about exploitation and researcher accountability.

The controversies also coincided with broader political struggles. During the late twentieth century, the Yanomami faced land grabs, disease outbreaks, and pressures from gold mining. How anthropologists portrayed them affected policy and public perception. Depictions of them as violent "Stone Age" warriors undermined their claims to land rights, while portrayals as victims of ethnocide bolstered international solidarity campaigns. In all this, the voices of the Yanomami themselves were rarely heard.

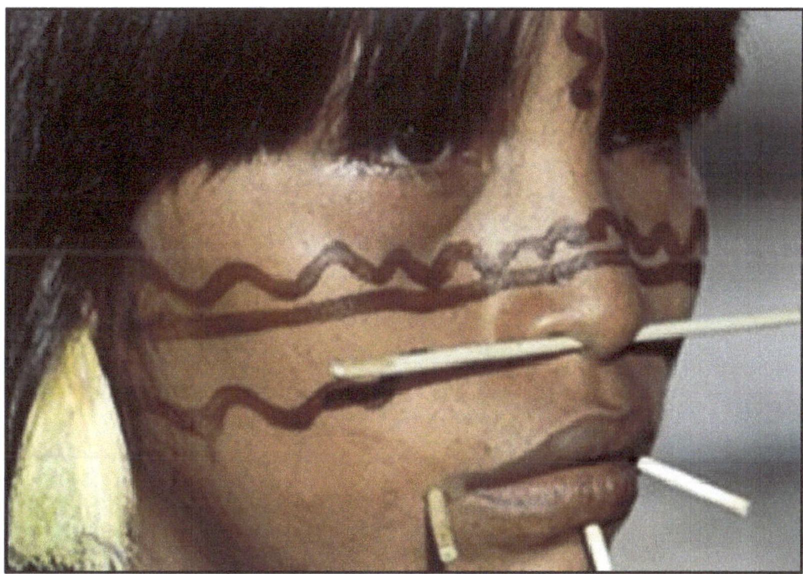

Yanomami girl

The TV programme I'd watched failed to acknowledge their achievements. Chagnon's claim to fame is in tracing lineages and mapping social linkages. Warfare and the stealing of women resulted in early death amongst the men and complex mixing of the gene pool. Chagnon's problem was that it is taboo amongst the Yanomani to name the dead. He overcame this difficulty by living with the people over many years and by carefully following clues in everyday conversations. Jacques achievement was to explore the mythical and complex spiritual world of the Yanomami. They practice shamanism and take drugs to achieve a hallucinogenic state in which they take on the personality and, they imagine, the physical form of wild animals and birds.

Today, the work of Lizot and Chagnon is both foundational and fraught. Their ethnographies remain widely cited in classrooms and scholarship, but most anthropologists would be critical of Chagnon's assertion that Yanomami aggression was rooted in biological differences and natural selection and of Lizot's alleged sexual exploitation of minors.

Helena Valero

I met Helena Valero in 1981 in Santa Elena de Uairén after Scharlie and I

Helena Valero with her father, second husband Akawe and children. C.1956-7

climbed Roraima.

Around age 12 (circa 1932), Helena Valero was kidnapped by the Kohorochiwetari, a Yanomami subgroup, after her family was attacked on the banks of the Maricoabi stream in the Brazilian Amazon. She survived being wounded during the ambush and, was left hidden while the rest of the family fled. Over the next twenty years, Helena lived among multiple Yanomami tribes—including the Kawawetari, Shamateri, and Namoeteri—being married twice and bearing four children.

In 1956, she escaped with her children and her second husband, Akawe, making contact with a logger who helped her reach San Fernando de Atabapo. There, she reunited with her younger brother and later her father. However, among her original family and in broader society, she faced rejection—discrimination due to her mixed identity and children of "mixed blood," along with severe poverty at a mission. Feeling alienated and out of place, she chose to return to Yanomami life, where, despite the challenges, she felt a more profound sense of belonging.

Her story was first told through Italian anthropologist Ettore Biocca, who recorded her oral testimonies in the early 1960s and wrote *Yanoáma: dal*

Helena Valero c.1981

racconto di una donna rapita dagli Indi (1965). A revised Spanish-language version – *Yo soy Napëyoma. Relato de una mujer raptada por los* indígenas *yanomami* – was published in the early 1980s.

Helena Valero was a remarkable women, using her wit, intelligence and sociability to survive multiple attempts on her life. I remember her telling me how a woman could divorce her husband if she met another man but the husband had the right to dissolve the marriage by hitting her over the head with a thick pole of macana wood. Notably, anthropologists consider her narrative authentic and invaluable because her stories derive from lived experience. Helena Valero's life provides rare insight into Yanomami culture at a time before modern contact and external influence. She reportedly said that the Yanomami were "neither devils nor angels, but human like the rest of us," challenging romanticised or demonised views of indigenous cultures. Her narrative is valuable for the simple reason that Helena was there as a member of this society.

Araguaney (Handroanthus chrysanthus) national tree of Venezuela